Momma's Boy Gone Bad

poems by

William A. Greenfield

Finishing Line Press
Georgetown, Kentucky

Momma's Boy Gone Bad

Copyright © 2017 by William A. Greenfield
ISBN 978-1-63534-132-4 First Edition
All rights reserved under International and Pan-American Copyright Conventions.
No part of this book may be reproduced in any manner whatsoever without written permission from the publisher, except in the case of brief quotations embodied in critical articles and reviews.

ACKNOWLEDGMENTS

Deep appreciation is given to the editors of the following publications where versions of these poems have appeared or have been accepted for publication.
"Left Lane Ends" appeared in *The Barbaric Yawp.*
"Dusk" appeared in *The East Coast Literary Review, The Bookends Review* and *The Tower Journal.*
"Birdman" appeared in *The Storyteller Magazine, The Artistic Muse* and *The Tower Journal.*
"Not Recommended for Full Sun" appeared in *The Front Porch Review.*
"Momma's Boy Gone Bad" appeared in *The Bookends Review, Down in the Dirt Magazine, Stepping Stones Magazine* and *The Tower Journal.*
"Reverb" has been accepted for publication in *2 Bridges Review.*
"Pictorial" and "RAM" appeared in *The Tower Journal.*
"Manitoba" and "The Ever Shrinking Universe" appeared in *The Westchester Review.*
"My Father's Shoes"appeared in *The Bookends Review.*
"Fraud" and "Why I Love the Wind" appeared in *The Linnet's Wings.*
"Segue"appeared in *The Black Fox Literary Magazine.*
"The Value of X" appeared in *The Magnolia Review.*
"First Love" appeared in *Carve Magazine.*
"Going South"appeared in *The Emerge Literary Journal*
"Dirty Old Men" and "Eagles Nest" appeared in T*he East Jasmine Review*

Sincerest thanks go out to my daughter, Sonia Greenfield, for her support and guidance.

Publisher: Leah Maines
Editor: Christen Kincaid
Cover Art: William A. Greenfield
Author Photo: Nancy Greenfield
Cover Design: Elizabeth Maines

Printed in the USA on acid-free paper.
Order online: www.finishinglinepress.com
also available on amazon.com

Author inquiries and mail orders:
Finishing Line Press
P. O. Box 1626
Georgetown, Kentucky 40324
U. S. A.

Table of Contents

First Love 1
From Where I Lie 2
Left Lane Ends 3
Dirty Old Men 4
Birdman 5
RAM 6
Momma's Boy Gone Bad 7
Manitoba 8
Sky Dancing 9
Pictorial 10
The Ever Shrinking Universe 12
Reverb 13
Segue 14
The Value of X 15
Nestled 16
Fraud 18
Not Recommended for Full Sun 19
My Father's Shoes 20
Why I Love the Wind 22
Dusk 23
Eagle's Nest 24
Going South 25
A Child's Unfinished Symphony 26

First Love

Mint leaves covered a rusty fence,
separating yards and strings
from the heart.
Folding a leaf between
thumbs, I forced a sound
not unlike a shofar's *tekia*.
If not minding siblings, she
would come, take my hand
and pretend to tell my fortune.
One Saturday, she heeded
the piping, took me behind
her father's garage and revealed
her pre-pubescent parts.
An eternal pact I presumed,
something never to be broken.
We were so *convenient*.
We shared the same view of
Mr. Cole's market. We heard
the same firehouse siren
at 5:00 each day.
I came to know that
not every first finger entwined
or every first quiver of loins
will blossom. There are
things more enticing than
rusty fences or the boy
next door. And I know that
this is, of course, how it
always should be.

From Where I Lie

Her rhythmic breathing has settled in
ever so rapidly; a melody amongst dissonance,
reassuring yet baffling. She finished painting
the bedroom today. She aches yet
smiles smugly in her sleep. Yesterday
was so routine in the light of day.
Yesterday, the woes of those I touched
were without consequence, like reading
a stranger's obituary. Now I recite
sermons over and over, arguments I should
have used yesterday. Now, I expose myself
to the whirl of a ceiling fan and struggle
to find comfort by defeating the winds that chill.
Tiny percussion plays against the window and the
tiny spider on the ceiling politely keeps his distance.
Everything is amplified; everything a distraction.
Sparks fly from the plow making its third round.
She stirs just slightly as I reach for the puzzle book.
A streak in her hair matches the *toasted pine nut*
that covers the walls. Old men with worldly
responsibilities are content. Old men smile
smugly in their sleep. One eye on the spider,
one eye on the pillbox, as I envy the things
around me that always seem to work just right
from where I lie.

Left Lane Ends

Heading west on the interstate,
unsure whether the radio
was entertainment or a distraction.
Mirror sunglasses in the mirror
let me look at myself without
looking too far inside.
reflections just casting a
distorted image of sky and pavement,
but not the finite pith I could
find inside
dirty snow on the shoulder,
soon to be hidden by the coming
nor'easter; soon to be buried and
never seen again
just the dirt left behind when spring
sends the big machines to the warehouse
Cones and flashers signal a
new pattern from the old way
to the new way; pushing me
to the right,
squeezing me.
nowhere left to go

Dirty Old Men

They may, in fact, be soiled.
They may have dirt beneath
their nails, under their chin,
on the fingers of their gloves.
And their shovels and stones
have become heavy, like
their eyelids in the late
afternoon. Old is relative
to them, as there is always
someone older and dirtier,
someone who uses a cane
or someone who carries
oxygen around. They can
smile politely at the waitress,
but eye contact must be
brief and cloudy, like
watching the news
on a rainy day. The young
and supple reside only
in the dreams of when they
were not so old, when
their shirts were snug
and their eyes were clear
and wandering as they
swaggered up to the counter
flashing a dimple that
was anything but dirty.

Birdman

Dozens of blackbirds sat
on a wire above the horse farm.
I saw them see me.
I saw them jockey for position.
They didn't need to take flight,
didn't need to be capable;
no more capable than the
infant learning to babble,
learning to recognize, like
the blackbirds recognized me.
Beyond the horse farm
sat the charred remains:
just a foundation and chimney:
certainly a problem of
tangible proportions.
Just how much can ashes
weigh on the mind?
I don't recall what lay
beyond on that day. I was
thinking of a time long
ago, when I was bathing
my infant son. As
simple as they were,
his needs far outweighed
my own. A day came
when he asked if he
had become a man, I
had no answer, as I
know only when a man
is no longer a man, when
he becomes a nucleus
of blood and bone, watching
with indifference as the world
revolves around him, like the
blackbirds watched me on
that day, from their lofty perch
high above the horse farm.

RAM

There was an actor I saw
years ago battling dinosaurs
on *Million Dollar Movie*.
Now I see his face at four a.m.
and I can't remember his name;
so I pace from room to room
because I can't *Google* a face.
Why should I really give a
rat's ass about matching a
face with a name. I keep
repeating this while I
hyperventilate. I pick up
my crosswords only
because the answers are
handy. Answers are calming.
I once read that being left off
the A-list could send a socialite
into a similar frenzy. I try
to bury the pieces; the name
of the kid that sat next to me
in chemistry class, the girl
throwing up on the playground.
Why can't I bury these useless
glimpses? Why does four a.m.
trigger this hemorrhaging of
panic, when trying to grasp the
details of a fading dream is
like trying to grasp loose stones
on a slippery slope. I have no
answers. I have only a
convenient escape route.
The light of day will arrive soon,
with all of its clarity. I will see
a friend at the firehouse barbeque
and make a note of his name
for future reference.

Momma's Boy Gone Bad

Dear Mother
I am sorry for not coming to visit you,
for not sitting cross-legged in the open field
while reciting confessions. I am sorry
you cannot count my thousand thanks
for the many model trains and superheroes
that drove the family debt to somewhere
between impossible and my father's insanity.
I should have leapt from my bed and came
to your defense late at night when you
screamed at him, demanding the car keys
because you "just wanted to go for a ride".
I now confess mother. It wasn't the heroes
I craved. It was you I wanted, not to be shared
with brothers or sisters, just you and me
having French toast in the diner
on Sunday morning, you and me on a train ride
to the city, your voice singing Nature Boy
only to me. I am sorry that you denied yourself
baubles and furs. But I now understand
why you feared the dark, why the TV
stayed on all night, why you couldn't make
the briefest trip to the nearby market. Someday
I will bite back on my own fears and come
to visit you. I suppose we could reminisce
about model trains. I could try to explain
why there is a machine next to me at
bed time, recycling white noise like
an old TV after the anthem has concluded.

Manitoba

I saw it snow
in early June on Lake Kississing.
I was alone but I was not lonely,
as I might be at rush hour
on the IRT. The loons dove
swiftly at my approach and I
searched the dark waters,
wondering where they would
reappear and sing to me again.
Nearly midnight and I could
still see the black worm-earth
that coated my fingertips.
The echoes were entertaining
but somehow thoughtless,
as if I were speaking loud
profanities at the public library.
A single beacon of light from miles
away guides me home, crude
and simple as it may be.
I thought that it would not
be so terrible to die here.
And when I doused the
guiding flame, the jewels
of Orion were never
so wondrous.

Sky Dancing

the rustling from a distance
and the wind that comes
is a young thing
newly wrought and pristine
a treetop performance
of the June Taylor dancers
at prime time
betraying each other's
movements like a perchance
near collision of strangers
on a busy sidewalk
a green on blue
collage of undulation
and whispers from the sky

Pictorial

I used to look through books of pictures

elderly women in summer dresses
my mother as a young lady
smoking Lucky Strikes in a diner
faded pencil remarks
a year and a town
I had an Aunt Lily who once
sent me a harmonica from Philadelphia
overcoats and a '53 Packard
a soldier in sunglasses

I used to look through books of pictures

third shelf from the top
a jet plane called a *Banshee*
the incredibly long Diplodocus
the U.S. Naval Fleet
diesel engines
through a mountain pass
howitzers
bazookas
and other killing machines

I used to look through books of pictures

I was holding a model car
crying in the funhouse
in my mother's arms with a box of Sugar Pops
on a pony in a cowboy hat
knee deep with a bucket and shovel
under the big maple with Diana
and my new harmonica

I used to look through books of pictures

dog ears
strange shoes
and dead people

The Ever Shrinking Universe

So I come padding out of the bedroom
in manly slippers and she says "Yo Baby."
We do this silly fist bump thing and
I ask,
"*Djeet?*" She says "Cheerios."
There's
much to do, so we plan.
She'll drive down
and I'll drive back.
Now we're outside
Hallmark
eating marshmallow Santas and
she asks why we still laugh. I
explain
that the world gets smaller
everyday.
There is no room left
for suicide bombers,
federal deficits,
troubled souls.
She remembers
that we have to
get a card and send money
to the paperboy, but I put that
thought
behind me because I
can't find my way out
of J.C. Penny's.
She laughs those pathetic
tears and
takes my hand. "Well," I say,
"the store is just too big." So, we shrink
down, our world a snow globe. Shaken,
it's nothing but a swirl of flakes. Wound up,
we hear nothing but a twinkle
of mirth.

Reverb

It may have started when
you caught a riff or a catchy
lyric while feeding your head.
Or maybe you were groping
down some lover's lane during
the British invasion. Somehow,
you got hooked, and from that
day forward it's all surreal.
You see him as a genius who
sings just for you. You've lost
count of the trips to The Garden
and The Coliseum. Someday
you will have to reconcile. He will
grow old and become obscure and
he will die. You will sob like a baby
and rationalize that's it's not like
those nut jobs that needed
therapy after Lennon was slain.
And then you will slide a CD in,
turn to your wife of many years
and say "this is vintage" and hope
she doesn't mock your pathos.
You listen and remember the
perfect rainbow from yesterday
that rose from the horizon like
a giant candy stick. Like the segue
from track two, you had no one
to share it with. Again, you must
reconcile. Reverberations are like
people. They decrease in amplitude
over time until they reach zero.

Segue

being enamored to things;
the taste of cinnamon and blueberries,
the red beginning to flourish
on laden branches along the highway,
a scent left on her bed clothes

But, in the end,
it is the long conceptual composition.
A crescendo
sets my nape hairs to bristle
as it takes me full circle
to a melody that ends
just as it began.

In the end, given the warmth
of her hand in mine, it is
these melodies I will miss the most.

The Value of X

will never be the capitol of New Jersey
or a signature on the Magna Carta.
X will never equate
to internal combustion
or something shaped
and molded
by talented young hands,
will never be built
with sand and mortar.
The value of x
is part of an obtuse world,
beyond the grasp
of the creative mind
that draws an intricate butterfly
on a piece of scrap,
that creates a complex circuit
of wires or words.
The value of x
cannot improve the arc
of a curve ball or
a three pointer.
Unlike
a rainbow's spectrum
or the brightest star you see,
the value of x
cannot be remembered.

Nestled

This thickening green
protects me and keeps me
insulated
like a chrysalis.
It keeps out the sobbing
of small children and
discontented rants.

It catches the falling skies
and later
when the mist weaves
through the ferns
the drip-drip lulls
like the grandfather clock
in the dark corner.

A butterfly made of cloth
twirls in unison to
the dancing hickory
and a canopy
of maple here and
there is breached and
splashes of light adorn
the forest floor.

The fluttering seems to come
from inside my head as
Starthroats appear from nowhere
to vie for nectar.
I have tried in vain to echo
the black-capped chickadee.
If only I could whistle like
my mother did.

I can no longer see
the mountains to the north or
the clapboard farmhouse to the west.
But this is a welcomed shroud
where, from within, it rains
whirlybirds of samaras
to germinate long after
I am gone.

Fraud

I have it all backwards,
not moved by the intricacies
of an autumn maple leaf,

not in awe of ocean surf,
no need or desire to describe
the dark closet of my childhood

home or the fear felt when
the air raid siren wailed.
No words burn so intense

that I must bare my soul,
so call me cold. But it is
something I've chosen to

create. A poem, the flower
I plant today to admire
tomorrow, the red striped tie

with the perfect windsor knot,
the final coat of varnish
on a scalloped picture frame.

Not Recommended for Full Sun

It was in the middle of spring when I concluded
that sunshine alone was not enough. Should I
be a beachcomber or a Virgin Mary's flower,
perhaps it would be sufficient. But I am not.
The sun must fall below a line of Ash and Maple
and lay down bars of shadow across an expanse
of green or paint something from an artist's
rendition; a farmhouse where a rocking chair
sits unoccupied but so very inviting.
There must be contrast, like a tan line across
an expanse of supple skin. There must be a
single point of dazzling light in a half full glass
of Chardonnay. There must be hummingbirds
that I hear before I see and shadows that I see
before the darkness takes it all away.

My Father's Shoes

Hand- me- overs from a learned brother,
they lay cracked and misshapen
in the bottom of the dark closet;
a symbol of some latent sadness.
It was there, but hidden from
the innocence of youth.
They spoke of a man in need of
something above and beyond the
benefits of comfortable footwear.

I can remember his facts.
He never drank milk.
He denied my sister a trip
to the shoe store in the snow.
He wouldn't say why, couldn't reveal
the fear, the compassion. He was
unable or unwilling to console his wife
when her anxiety surfaced late at night.
So, he would do deeds for the needy.

I worked with him in the summer
for a rich uncle. He sometimes
used the "F" word to impress me; to
make me less innocent and a bit more
brazen. He told me he was a bad example
of what I could become. I never knew
if he had expectations. But there were
requirements, like taking out the garbage
and sweeping the porch.

I don't recall if his widow mourned
when his damaged heart could do no more.
I don't remember tears of grief. I remember
pictures of a soldier in sunglasses and
lectures about returning a screwdriver.

I should have asked if there was more;
something I could do when a firm handshake
was just not enough to fill an empty
pair of second hand shoes

Why I Love the Wind

The wind is something new,
consummated by the gods
to bring me the scent of pine,
is something I can balance on
my shoulders like an infant
at the fair, not so heavy as to
weigh me down, but there
to remind me

of things still living as dead
leaves skitter in its wake, as
maple saplings bend to its
power.

Let it set the walls to quake
and raise the settled dust,
and I will celebrate its birth
and listen

to all the songs the wind
can play.

Dusk

There is an ebbing of spirit;
the part that marvels at a sailor's sunset
or finds solitude in the noise that crickets make.
In the coming twilight I will perform a life sustaining
walk past rolling leas and century
old farm houses. My arms and legs will
function like the involuntary beating of a heart.
I do hope that one day soon
a resolute spirit will resurface;
one that yearns fascination, like those
that come and flutter their powdered wings
seeking but a brief respite from the darkness,
one that can laugh along with a farmer's
children at the morning bus stop,
one that can acquiesce to the
fading light of days.

Eagle's Nest

The skateboarder gracefully slaloms
around the gas pumps at the local Valero;
this *Road Warrior* in a desolate
world that offers little
beyond smooth asphalt
and a limber joystick. His mother
wraps her arms around
herself like the wings
of an eagle ready to soar so
high that the world becomes
miniature. She could scan
the countryside for choice worms
to wriggle their way into his brain
and one day make him capable,
make him different than her,
make him healthy. He has
a sickness that permeated
from a nest where tiercels
came and went but never
fed him a morsel, never soared
into the vacuum with his mother.
So she hugs herself and calls
the medi-van, claiming her
body is swollen, claiming
that his intellect blocks
the ability to ask for help.
Yesterday he climbed
to the roof and slept like
a vagrant in the rail yard.
He dreamt that he could fly.

Going South

The hydrangea
blossoms slump to
the wet grass each morning,
like old men
whose own weight
has become
too much to bear.
The goldfinch
will soon be gone.
Still,
there are many
things to care for;
the perennial
daisies to be
tucked in,
knuckles that bleed,
fingers that turn
ghostly white.
But I do not
fear
the cold as much
as I fear the
need
to escape
from it, like
a scared rabbit burrowing
deep to
escape a raptor's talons.

A Child's Unfinished Symphony

There is a pounding
bass inside of
his head
sometimes it comes
from his earbuds
sometimes it's the sound
of his grandfather slumping
to the kitchen floor as all
the love and wisdom
vanished with the last
beat of his heart
his mother's cry
a shrill cacophony
as his anger misplaced
brings her to tears
while recovery
teeters like the
soccer ball balanced
in the balance between
what is good and
the dead that left
him empty
cut off like a
CD with no more
room for the
crescendo he could
be like Jimmy's
navigation of the
Stairway

William A. Greenfield grew up some forty miles north of New York City in the small hamlet of Montrose, New York, where he learned how to play baseball, climb trees, and make change at the local supermarket. He first began to write poetry while attending the State University of New York at Plattsburgh. For years after that, his writing became only an occasional dabbling. At the urging of his daughter, he once again delved into the world of poetry in more recent years to the point where it became a regular part of his existence. His poems can be found in numerous journals including *The Westchester Review, Carve Magazine, The East Coast Literary Review* and many others. In 2012 he won Storyteller Magazine's People's Choice Award. He resides in Sullivan County, New York in the middle of the woods and he likes it there.

www.ingramcontent.com/pod-product-compliance
Lightning Source LLC
LaVergne TN
LVHW041519070426
835507LV00012B/1690